Stephen Knight was born in Swansea, and there are many references to Wales in his poems. He studied English at Oxford University and trained as a director at the Old Vic Theatre School. He has written three prize-winning books of poetry, *Flowering Limbs*, *Dream City Cinema* and *The Sandfields Baudelaire*, and one novel, *Mr Schnitzel*, for adults. This is his first collection for younger readers. He teaches creative writing at a number of colleges and universities and lives just outside London with his wife and daughter.

*Also from Young Picador*

OVERHEARD ON A SALTMARSH
Poems edited by Carol Ann Duffy

ONCE IN A HOUSE ON FIRE
Andrea Ashworth

THE PEACOCK SPRING
Rumer Godden

THE GREENGAGE SUMMER
Rumer Godden

MY HEARTBEAT
Garret Freymann-Weyr

MANY STONES
Carolyn Coman

WHEN KAMBIA ELAINE FLEW IN FROM NEPTUNE
Lori Aurelia Williams

# SARDINES
## AND OTHER POEMS

STEPHEN KNIGHT

YOUNG PICADOR

First published 2004 by Young Picador

This edition published 2005 by Young Picador
an imprint of Pan Macmillan Limited
20 New Wharf Road, London N1 9RR
Basingstoke and Oxford
www.panmacmillan.com

Associated companies throughout the world

ISBN 0 330 41356 2

Copyright © Stephen Knight 2004

The right of Stephen Knight to be identified as the
author of this book has been asserted by him in accordance
with the Copyright, Designs and Patents Act 1988.

All rights reserved. No part of this publication may be
reproduced, stored in or introduced into a retrieval system, or
transmitted, in any form, or by any means (electronic, mechanical,
photocopying, recording or otherwise) without the prior written
permission of the publisher. Any person who does any unauthorized
act in relation to this publication may be liable to criminal prosecution
and civil claims for damages.

1 3 5 7 9 8 6 4 2

A CIP catalogue record for this book is available from the British Library.

Printed by Mackays of Chatham plc, Chatham, Kent.

This book is sold subject to the condition that it shall not,
by way of trade or otherwise, be lent, re-sold, hired out,
or otherwise circulated without the publisher's prior consent
in any form of binding or cover other than that in
which it is published and without a similar condition including
this condition being imposed on the subsequent purchaser.

# ACKNOWLEDGEMENTS

*New Welsh Review, The North, Planet, Poetry London, Poetry Wales, Times Literary Supplement; Bonkers for Conkers* (Macmillan, 2003), *Mice on Ice* (Macmillan, 2004)

'After Dark' is a response to a painting of the same name by James Rielly. It was commissioned in 2000 by Sally Baker of Tŷ Newydd and Martin Barlow of Oriel Mostyn Gallery, Llandudno, in 2000.

'The Long Way Home' won the 2003 *TLS*/Blackwells Poetry Competition.

Thanks to Gaby Morgan, without whom this book wouldn't exist; to Amanda Dalton, for the Cuban melodious finches; and to Kate, these poems' first reader.

*For Sylvie*

# CONTENTS

# CONTENTS

# Nights

# Sardines

You slip behind your parents' clothes
 in nineteen sixty-eight,
pull shut the wardrobe door, then
 curl into a ball.
     You wait.

It's very still in there. So quiet.
 Your chin rests on your knees.
A long fur-coat is tickling
 so much you want to sneeze.

A year goes by. Neil Armstrong walks
 the surface of the moon
as slow as honey, while you think
 'Someone will find me soon!'

You fiddle with your father's ties.
 The earth crawls round the sun
and footsteps pass the wardrobe door.
 – It could be anyone!

The world outside turns decimal
 and all the old coins go
the way of dinosaurs, of early
 morning mist, of snow.

1

It's very quiet in there. So still.
    Your knees support your chin
while you whisper, 'Any minute now
    someone will burst in . . .'

Fashions change: hemlines fall and rise.
    Hands sometimes reach inside
to take a shirt or dress away –
    the door is opened wide

and then it's closed, and then it's dark
    once more. Leaves grow. Leaves fall.
The earth crawls round the sun again.
    (You almost *hear* it crawl.)

One day in nineteen eighty-five
    you think about your life
alone; but there's room for neither
    children nor a wife

in there. It's very still. So quiet.
    Your chin rests on your knees.
Sometimes you whistle in that dark
    like wind through broken trees.

'No one's going to find,' you say,
    'my perfect hiding-place.
Not now.' It's nineteen ninety-nine.
    The planet spins through space,

the trees grow fat with overcoats
    and you, you droop until
(at last) you fall asleep.
                  Good night.
It's quiet in there, and still.
So still.
      So very still.

# Days

# The Long Grass

I lost my favourite football
in the long grass
thirty years ago.
We searched for hours,
for days, for weeks on end.
But could we find it? No.
The air will have escaped by now.

The fountain pen
my brother gave me
disappeared back then,
left for a moment;
but I can't remember
where or when.
Who waved a magic wand?

Somewhere between the front door
and eternity
I lost a bunch of keys.
Climbed on chairs to search for them.
Searched on hands and knees.
I asked my friends.
They have no news.

The wallet
given as a Christmas present?
Gone.
Gone with all its money
and the scraps of paper I had written on.
Will someone ever
hand it in?

I misplace people's names.
Their faces I remember, yes,
but who they are
and when we met
I cannot even guess.
My memory is decomposing
in the grass.

My toys have gone.
The diary I kept
when I was seventeen:
its list of favourite films,
the dreams of who I might have been.
Could they have wound up
in the bin?

With one, brief chapter
left to read
I left my book
somewhere sensible.
I've no idea where.
Will you help me look?
I can tell you what each character is like.

I miss my father, too.
I'd like to find him
but I don't know how.
Perhaps he's wading
through the long grass even now,
calling our names;
trying to get home.

# Late July

What happens when the gates are locked
and summer starts, beyond the playground's
chain-link fence, that famous puddle
dry in the centre circle, and blades of grass
back in the goalmouths worn to mud
all term, a solitary sick-note
fading on a staffroom window sill,
the registers completed for another year?

The long days hang from us like stones.
They drag us to the earth. They make us sleep.
And while we sleep, our voices break,
our faces change, our clothes tear at the seams.
We are lost in fields, in woods, in towns.
We will never be the same again.

# Our Visitor, the Rain

is always looking for a place to live,
commuting through gutters, renting our drains:

I have (he thunders) so much to give,
tending the gardens, scrubbing the roads, soaking
your clothing and washing your feet . . .
And so he rains and rains and rains.

He knows we know he's only joking –
How very funny! we should say, How sweet!

I've heard we're made of water anyway.
Who cares about a little rain
visiting like a relative now and again
to stay for an hour, perhaps, or else a day?

We couldn't live without him, after all,
so,

    let him drench us
    let him bathe us
    let him douse us
    let him splash us
    let him fall . . .

# Now He is Burying the Car

I'm burying my parents' car
　　on Caswell Beach. I have
my plastic spade – so far
　　it's taken me one day

to excavate the hole (I've had
　　some help from suntanned men
who tell me I am mad).
　　'I'm not,' I say, 'I'm not.'

I gather up some seaweed
　　now, to decorate the mound.
How many strands I'll need
　　is not decided yet.

And when I'm good and ready
　　I'll roll the car along
the beach. The men will wave to me,
　　their children laugh and shout.

Goodbye to nodding dogs (I'll chant)
　　Goodbye to seat belts too –
if someone shouts, 'You can't
　　do this!', I'll answer, 'Yes, I can.'

Imagine all that sand strapped in
   till Kingdom-come,
the wheels that will not spin
   again, the engine choked with gold!

And when the waves arrive
   to soak through all that sand,
rust will thrive,
   the mound will disappear . . .

It's boiling now. There's not a cloud
   in sight. No mam to wail, no dad
to say, 'It's not allowed,
   this burying of cars. You're mad!'

I wonder where they are.

# Between Two Hands

When was I last between two hands,
my mother's and my father's hands
lifting me towards the sky
or trawling me across the sands?

– The future slipped away: the rough,
the smooth. Their mighty hands,
their faces near the sun. The shouting one.
The one who understands.

When did they do my buttons up?
The perfect, silver ones. Or tie
the laces of my shoes?
Or swing me till I kicked the sky?

When was I last between two hands,
alive at every fingertip
until they tore me down the middle
like a pink Permission slip?

14

# The Adracabadra Man

Here comes the final act,
the man whose face is pale, whose smile is cracked.
The auditorium is packed.

A deck of cards falls from his hands –
ace upon ace upon ace lands
face up, where he stands

in something like despair,
trying to pluck a rabbit from the air.
Nothing's there.

He should be in a rage,
pulling a cloth from off an empty cage.
We watch him watch one bunny hop across the stage.

The front row leaves
when, oops, his doves explode from both his sleeves.
Bereft, he grieves;

but then (I'm telling you, it's true)
he starts to saw his sparkly wife in two.
Oh dear. A very, very, VERY messy thing to do.

# The Loved Ones

Perhaps we played outside
all afternoon, climbing the slide
while they stole away
 . . . it must be years and years ago;
and, busy growing up,
we were slow to ask our parents
exactly when they left for ever.

– What happened then?
Perhaps they haunted
Ravenhill Park for days on end
then shuffled home to lie
awake all night, knitting
unwanted socks.

If brooches, clocks, linen
or best china reach us
years later we remember
all their fussing
when we were three years old.
Those thin hands we held
(Forgive us) so reluctantly.
Their crumpled skin.

Or else we apologize,
smile even,
because we can't begin to testify
how wise they were, how fierce;
because we can't recall
the colour of their eyes.

We had an orange ball:
we used to laugh:
we used to sing and shout:
and if we thought at all
we had no doubt.

Perhaps we played outside.
Perhaps the sun was out.

# The Dog in Double Geography

From somewhere in the last years of my childhood,
a dog is barking. One sunny afternoon in May
an hour before the end of lessons that day.
A geography test. I am no good.

He might be trapped four floors below
(my school is very tall, I'm at the very top)
but I am wishing he could stop
or simply go.

A map of somewhere drawn with coloured chalks:
blue for water, brown for contours, the rest in white.
If I can only think, everything will be all right.
Despite the barking, no one talks.

I'm sorry, Sir, I could not pass your test.
A dog was calling, calling me to go
and find him where he lay, four floors below.
I tried my best –

the problem wasn't you, but me,
up here, overlooking the sun-dark places
where I lost my school friends' names and faces;
where a dog is barking, endlessly.

# Where the Circus is Now

In this bare field, my daughter stands
to show me where the lions roared;
the dents their cages made
still visible; the tracks
a worried lion-tamer left behind.

'And here,' she says, 'the bareback riders
rode their horses round the ring,'
then points to where they galloped.
'And this,' she says, 'is where I sat.'

The shops take last month's posters down.
The grass is worn to nothing,
here and there, though where we are
new blades come through

and there my daughter is,
her head tipped back to face the sky,
showing me how the lions roared.

# The Missing

Our heads appear on posters.
Our parents meet reporters.

Reporters ask our neighbours
questions they can't answer.

Our neighbours hug their children
and lock them in each evening.

Children wear our clothing
then walk the paths we travelled.

We pass the shopping centre's
cameras, high above us.

A moment. When we vanish,
our heads appear on posters.

*

The streets on which we played
forget us altogether.

The houses where we lived
go quiet, like museums.

20

The rooms in which we slept
remain the way we left them.

Our parents visit, every day,
the dolls, the cricket bats,

the wardrobe full of clothes
we grow too old for, somewhere.

Our homework books preserve
essay plans, unsolved equations.

# *You Are My Sunshine*

The lass on a bench in Leatherhead Park,
a warm hat, a handbag, wintry clothes
and the auburn beard – this made me start! –
of an out-of-season Santa Claus,
knitting a long, inexplicable scarf
which grew towards her toes.

Trees hung heavy with the weight of summer.
My sleeves rolled up, my tie and jacket gone,
I listened from my bench beside the pond
while she murmured a beautiful song
and pinball insects skimmed the water,
ignorant of the perpendicular.

# Work Work Work

Even now, they excavate
the ground beneath our feet.
They take to bits the very street.
They work until it's late.

The soil becomes a powder
heaped between the paving-stones.
Listen to their little groans –
higher pitched, now; louder.

What tunnels there must be
down there, what halls, what giant
chambers where the meek and pliant
serve their queen eternally.

But if they should decide
it's much too dark down there
– down there in all that loamy air –
then come from far and wide

to colonize our places,
it won't be long before we sound
like them, push balls of dirt around
and live life underground

while ant masks pinch our faces.

# The Boy Who Can't Get Out of Bed

is me.

The kid who draws
his curtains tight
on perfect afternoons
despite the heat

is me.

The lad whose pillow
keeps that hole
a head will leave
if left too long

is me.

The yob who speaks
in grunts, then dips
beneath the duvet
like a mole

is me.

The nipper's eyes
unused to light?
Whose pasty skin
could pass for milk?

Both mine.

The urchin told
his arms and legs
resemble strings?
That puny one

is me.

The boy whose parents
change entirely
downstairs, while he
is cast adrift

is me.

I will not move.
I will not change.
I will not leave
my bed; my bed

is me
is me
is me.

25

# On Your Marks

The number 8 stepped up
to take his penalty in 1973.
I'm crouching now, my arms apart.
Back then, I wasn't ready.

The things I built that fell to bits?
At last, I own the proper tools.
Those interviews that didn't work?
I have the answers. All of them.

She told me I was not
the one, ten years ago last February.
Here are the flowers. Here's the ring.
Back then, I wasn't ready.

The photographs I didn't take?
My camera's pressed against my face.
The places I have never seen?
My passport's here, in front of me.

Two years ago, I lost my dad.
I reached his side too late
for one last word. My mouth is dry,
and still I am not ready.

# The World's Worst Escapologist

moved in next door to us last year.
Now, 254
milk bottles sit, unclaimed, outside his door.
I wonder why we haven't seen him yet.

# Covering Your Eyes,

they spin you round and round
until you almost fall;
and then it seems they leave
without a sound

so, turning anywhere
and everywhere to find
someone, you only catch
armfuls of air.

Your fingers brush the wall
or sniff the air like worms.
Afraid to move too much,
you're feeling small.

There's traffic roaring far
away, while silence (here,
with you) is something quite
particular.

You're trapped here, with the sea;
you hear it whispering.
The sea, or else the wind
around a tree.

Your fingers touch the door
– its handle round and cold,
it's wooden skin lukewarm –
then stroke the floor.

Nothing stirs. Not a thing –
well, a spider hammers
a new web into place.
It's deafening!

Could any sound be worse?
A buzzing, glue-soaked fly?
Or no one else in all
the universe

but you, alone? Your heart
so loud it might explode?
Your head tipped back? Your long
arms miles apart?

# The Chosen

Our backs against the fence,
   we're waiting to be picked.
We fidget. We are tense.
   Our knees are very clean.

The tallest boy is chosen.
   The rain is in his eyes.
His arms and legs are frozen.
   He walks away from us.

The wind offends our necks.
   The field has turned to mud.
The boy beside me checks
   his shockproof diver's watch.

A second walks away,
   a third, and then a fourth
like minutes in a day.
   The raindrops tick and tock.

Our clothes are going rotten
   where we stand. The game we've come
to play is long forgotten.
   What happened to the goal?

And where's the stupid ball?
    And whose idea was it
to step outside at all?
    We bow our heads to pray.

Our T-shirts cling to us.
    Our boots are sopping wet.
We're waiting to be picked.
    It hasn't happened yet.

# An Awkward Customer
# Refuses to Buy the Weather

I will not purchase rain,
it only makes me wet.
Don't try to sell me frost.
It shatters underfoot.

Your snow? It's much too white,
too white, and strangely flat.
And as for all your wind?
I have enough of that.

# We Let the Fog Come In

Fog does not wipe its feet.
The fog that's coming in
is neither kind nor neat.

By covering the chairs
it's neither kind nor neat.
Fog slithers up the stairs.

To slip inside our beds,
fog slithers up the stairs.
Fog penetrates our heads.

Like something we once heard,
fog penetrates our heads –
like phrases, or a word

we cannot comprehend.
A phrase, or else a word.
A sentence with no end.

We let the fog begin
a sentence with no end.
We let the fog come in.

# The Winter House

Light bulbs are jewelled with frost,
icicles grow from the taps,
blizzards occur in the hall every day –
guests are, invariably, lost.

In a chair made of ice
she sits on her own,
knitting her snow drifts
or gloves for the mice.

Her daughter left home
as soon as she could –
her frostbitten fingers recovered, in time.
(Her handwritten letters are really quite good.)

She lives in a desert
and writes every day
to her mother, locked in winter
miles away.

34

# January 7

My father left us in the dead of winter.
Snow shut the door. Snow turned the key.
My father left us in the dead of winter.
Now I leave blank the pages of my diary.

# The Wrong Things I Have Done

are living here with me;
unlocking doors, whispering on the stairs
or watching too much TV.
They put their feet up on the chairs,
they leave their dirty dishes everywhere.
A smell hangs in the air.

On the way to school
I squeeze past them in the hall.
They laugh at me. I am a fool.
A few have grown quite tall
and gangly because they eat so well.
If only they didn't smell,

if only they'd leave me be –
the one who sniggers, the one who wears
my shoes. They're haunting me.
I've had a go at prayers
and promises, or pretending I don't care,
but there

they are, slouching, as a rule.
Generally, their manners appal:
they pick their noses, scratch, drool,
fart when friends come to call.
'One day soon, we'll tell.
Have this.'
                    They give me Hell.

# The Old Machinery of Winter

The snow and ice machine
processes through the heart of town
in search of all things green
to make them black or brown
then drape what's left in white.
White fumes fill the air.

Working through the night,
snowflakes furnish everywhere,
upholster garden hedges,
walls, the street. Snow swerves
to soften our world's sharp edges
by building curves.

All day, we stand around,
agog at every change
outside – the hollow sound
our voices make is strange –
or else we hold our breath inside.
Winter is our bride.

# The Bloody Hypnotist

pronounces you 'A dog!'
and there you are,
showing us your teeth
or bothering the car.

We walk you on a lead.
You curl up on the chair.
Slobber spoils our shoes.
Fur goes everywhere.

Don't cock your leg in school.
Don't snarl in Chemistry.
Those other things you do?
Nobody should see.

# The Dog with No Name

Is the dog on the beach
alone, crashing the waves
and racing along the strand?

She stops to peruse
a rock pool, cairns of seaweed,
a starfish dead on the sand.

The wind is filling our coats.
It roars in our ears. We listen,
but no one is calling her.

The dog is on the beach
alone, crashing the waves
and racing along the strand.

Digging holes or contemplating
distant boats, she sniffs,
and then she swims again.

She shakes the water off.
It sparkles in the light.
And then she finds a stick.

Why is the dog on the beach
alone, crashing the waves
and racing along the strand?

# The Long Way Home

I take the long way home –
   passing the unlit factory,
the burnt-out car abandoned
   months ago, the tree

too black with dirt to breathe
   – my satchel full of things
to do for Monday, then
   I see the swings

the kids are playing on,
   the spider's web, the slide;
I take the long way home
   to stay outside

as long as possible, until
   the clouds are red and pink
and everyone's forgotten me,
   or so I think

passing the bumpy pitch
   the far side of the park
'you should avoid at all costs
   after dark'

when older, taller boys emerge;
   I take the long way, though
it's late, now, and I'm singing
   every song I know

– with no one to correct me,
   I make up half the words,
walking through a town that has
   no people now, no birds

to sing with me, no shop
   to sell me sweets,
no aunts and uncles hunting me
   down moonlit streets.

Although it's very late,
   I take the long way back:
the road behind is lit,
   the road ahead is black.

# The Final Kick

Our only ball was lofted
beyond the keeper's fingertips,
high above the crossbar
and clear of the trees to finish
wallop! in the river
                              – before
we had a chance to bully
someone in the water, the current
took its trophy

downstream
towards the sea
where I believe
it's drifting even now
around the oceans of the world,
orbiting the planet like a brand-new moon.

# The Boy on the Roundabout

The gates chained. Litter spilling from a metal bin.
The wind is all that's there this evening,
racing round our playground in the middle of the park
in the hour of growing dark.
No one will let us in.

The swings are swinging empty in the breeze.
The see-saw and the rocking horse are still
in spite of all that careless air
circulating everywhere.
It scares the tallest trees

so much, they throw their leaves away . . .
I watched a boy too old to be there
turning on the roundabout this afternoon
while staring at a daylight moon.
Perhaps it was his final day.

When my time comes, I hope to know:
to know, and then to leave:
to turn my back on climbing frames and swings
and other childish things:
to close the gate: to look back once: then go.

# Silly Me

It was here a minute ago.
I left the room to make a cup of tea,
returned (drinking) and it had gone.
I put it there. Definitely.

No, it isn't in my pocket.
I didn't go upstairs. Or outside.
No one else has been here.
The door was not 'open wide'.

How can you misplace your childhood?
It's ridiculous. Something that big.
Has someone been up to no good?

The friends. The open spaces.
The new, unbroken things. Where are they?
My secrets. My games. The faces.

# The Song of the Trousers

*Carlos Avila, flying in from Havana,*
*was arrested in Miami airport after*
*customs officials found 44 songbirds,*
*including Cuban melodious finches,*
*hidden in his trousers. If convicted*
*of unlawful importation, he could*
*face five years in jail.*

> *Edinburgh Evening News*
> *15 November 2001*

The passenger singing
aloud, on the aisle,
does not move his lips –
not even to smile.

He looks rather shifty.
He shifts in his seat
or walks like a cowboy.
He stares at his feet.

(Birds nest in his pockets.
Birds perch on his knees.
They sing of the forest,
of missing the trees.)

That strangely-built man,
the passengers say,
never stops twitching.
He's twitched half the day.

He twitched in Havana,
he's twitched on the plane.
He scratches his backside.
It's been quite a strain.

(Birds nest in his pockets.
Birds perch on his knees.
They sing of the forest,
of missing the trees.)

He jumps from his seat
as he lets out a yelp.
An air hostess asks him
how she can help.

The trolley, he murmurs,
then purchases drinks
to pour on his trousers.
That's better, he thinks.

(Birds nest in his pockets.
Birds perch on his knees.
They sing of the forest,
of missing the trees.)

He's tortured by something
alive in his pants.
A medical problem?
An army of ants?

Oh, Señor Avila,
you look very ill.
Why do you wriggle?
Can't you keep still?

(Birds nest in his pockets.
Birds perch on his knees.
They sing of the forest,
of missing the trees.)

At last, in Arrivals,
he walks through the gate
cool-headed but gingerly.
Is it too late?

Pilots stop talking
to watch as he passes.
Officials, amazed, start
cleaning their glasses.

(Birds nest in his pockets.
Birds perch on his knees.
They sing of the forest,
of missing the trees.)

And then, birds erupt
half dead from his flies –
they flap to the ceiling
or race to the skies:

his trousers in tatters,
birds flap everywhere
relieved and excited
to be in the air,

birds pour from his pockets,
birds fly from his knees:
they sing of the forest,
of missing the trees.

So Carlos Avila's
transported to jail
to sing like those finches,
to warble and wail.

And Carlos, poor Carlos,
whose strategy failed,
sang like those finches,
warbled and wailed

while, deep in the forest,
birds perch in the trees
to sing of his trousers,
of missing his knees.

# Nights

# The Second Half

The old men wearing rags kicked off
in the summer of 1965.
The first was taken by a nasty cough,
a second by the flu; the third
expired without a word
at least ten years ago.
How many boys are left alive
and kicking? I don't know.
Out there, it's nearly dark
and they're still playing in the park.

Still playing football in the park,
they're well into the second half.
It started, back then, as a lark;
now, only illness makes them stop.
Their shoes are a holey disgrace!
Stiff-legged, they play at walking pace.
Sometimes, you hear them laugh
or swear; then shouting fills that space.
They may be old and fit to drop
but they are never going home.

# The Portmead Snowball

began
no bigger than your hand
one evening after school, outside
my classroom. I struggled, knee-deep in snow, to stand.

Creaking
like a rusted hinge, it rolled
along, gathering grit and grass,
stripping the playground of all its snow. I was cold

but still
I loved to watch it grow
so much; too much, perhaps, to curb
its appetite for reams and reams of perfect snow.

My breath
exploded from my face,
my lungs and legs began to ache
but still I had to push that snow from place to place,

around
the quiet, frozen streets
where no cars ventured out – it grew
in folds, in waist-thick ribbons, in serpentine pleats . . .

and squats
outside our house tonight
as big as any bus, so big
we're living in the dark all day, deprived of light.

In bed
I listen for the tick . . .
tick . . . tick of melting snow.

                              Slowly,
things emerge:

      dog leads

      pension books

      a walking stick

# The Far End of the Garden

His cup of tea is cold.
He must be, too.
The birds stopped singing hours ago.
The news is growing old
across his lap.

How can he stay out there?
The kitchen light
won't stretch as far as where he sleeps
in all that freezing air,
the grass so tall.

The night's long since begun.
Go call him in.
The deckchair cupped its hand for him
to face the setting sun,
but the sun has gone.

Here. Take a torch to find
your way to him,
I can't quite see him any more.
I'm sure he wouldn't mind.
Go bring him in.

# What Are You More Afraid Of?

A noise in the house
or no noise at all?
The instant before
or after the fall?

Fire or water?
In woods after dark
or alone in a boat?
A bear or a shark?

A river to cross
or a mountain to climb?
Saying goodbye with
too much or no time?

The breeze of your breath?
The knock of your heart?
Creatures that slither
or creatures that dart?

# Automacrosomatognosia

It's true – although I barely eat,
I grow another metre every night.
 . . . I could have said 'three feet',
give or take an inch, but that might
well have given you the wrong
idea! . . . I'm huge. I'm long.
I have a problem with my height.

I sleep with both legs poking through
my bedroom window now. My head
rests on the landing. Yes. It's true.
Four weeks ago, I broke my bed.
Now I can reach the tops of trees
in Brynmill Park. I'm scared. Please:
explain. Have I been overfed?

I hide inside our house all day.
No school will have me, not before
the growing stops for good. I weigh
as much as several cows, and roar,
in dreams, like King Kong. When I wake
I look to see what's left to break.
My clothes lie tattered on the floor –

these days I wear a striped marquee!
It won't be long before I'm left outside,
then birds will come to perch on me.
To build, to hatch. From far and wide.
At night, I'll stare at outer space
or rain will tumble down my face,
and there'll be nowhere left to hide.

*Automacrosomatognosia*: the conviction that the body is larger than it is

# What Happens in the Dark

There. Louder than before.
Scratching. Over there.

We shouldn't leave the fire.
We shouldn't stray too far

from here. Was that a car
outside? Or teeth and fur?

Dangerous and debonair,
equipped to bite and tear,

our neighbours' cats prepare
to take the midnight air.

They stop to say a prayer.
They cogitate. They stare.

It's cold. It's cold out there.
I do not think they care.

# After Dark

The six-year-old who lives next door
displays his fangs
in every family snap.
He's always neat,
always itching to explore
the corners of our town,
to map each novel street.

Insomniacs, we watch him
sneak between our houses in the early hours.
He spends the night
shaking trees,
making fences creak
or leaving trails of broken flowers
half his height.

How lonely it must be out there
pouncing with a squeaked 'I'VE GOT YOU'
while the dark
soaks everything and everywhere.
– Our precincts and our lawns
distilling dew;
our padlocked park.

# What I Did in the War

Raised voices.
Scraping chairs.
The smoke of battle
drifting
up the stairs.

Some anguish.
Some debris.
Nothing
but the darkness
next to me.

Downstairs
a slamming door,
a single cry.
Then silence,
as before.

Bloodied cushions.
Body parts.
The living
room a mess
of broken hearts.

One hole to keep
the dead.
I sleep inside
the deep
 trench of my bed.

# Signs of Life

Those little piles of droppings
   snug among your socks.
Scratches on the wardrobe door.
   Dead flies. Stopped clocks.

You hear their respiration
   menacing the night.
Hinges creak. The curtains move.
   Wake up. Turn on the light.

There's nothing there; and yet
   you have the strangest feeling.
Look up, then rub your eyes.
   Footprints on the ceiling.

# Red Flag Lullaby

The ocean bites, the ocean tears,
the ocean chews and gnaws,
my dear, don't go beyond your toes.

These waves make very little noise,
but they will do their worst.
Don't go beyond your knees

while birds are heading west
at some disturbing height.
Don't go beyond your waist.

By now, the waves will hurt –
they have that special knack.
Don't go beyond your heart,

my dear, to feel the water's knock.
Don't let the water lay you low,
don't go beyond your neck

tonight, don't let the fishes know
how far, how deep you have to go.
Don't go, my dear, don't go.

# The Last Boy in Captivity

parked, after dark,
alone but warm enough
among the boiled sweets
coated in fluff

I sleep
curled in the back seat
safe and sound
(a rug across my feet)

or breathe on the windscreen
then write my name.
When passing grown-ups stare
I do the same.

For company:
a wobbly gearstick,
a nodding dog,
a Batman comic.

And yet it's just too dark,
in here, to read
a thing. Shadows huddle
here, and feed

while street lights light my face.
The rear-view mirror has me
wide-eyed, like a goldfish
dreaming of the sea.

# The Astronaut's Complaint

We found, to our disgust,
its lakes and hills and seas
and steppes are made of dust;
and, no, there are no trees.

Our languid, lunar stroll
brought us face to face
with nothing. No beasts patrol
the lands of outer space,

no owls, no midnight cats
among the mountain tops,
no light-as-a-feather rats,
no cows, no sunlit crops.

If God *was* there, He's gone
and left a world of dust.
The whole thing is a con,
we learnt, to our disgust.

# A Saucerful of Milk

There she goes again, her cry
drifting upstairs near midnight;
so I leave my desk to find out why.

Perhaps it's food. I squeeze
a sachet of turkey into her bowl.
I call her, on my knees.

Biscuits? No, she has enough.
Company? She walks away,
banging the cat flap in a huff.

Then she's back to cry again.
I give her milk. She drinks.
(She has a saucerful, now and then.)

I rescued a bird from her claws
last week. Feathers turn up everywhere.
She is dangerous out of doors.

She is spiteful. She is cold.
Her eyes are blank. She will not
do as she is told.

Tomorrow, near midnight, her cry
will draw me downstairs.
Then, as now, I'll wonder why.

# Asleep,

somehow avoiding chairs
and walls, you leave your bed
to go alone downstairs.
You walk as if you're dead
and haunting us.

And when the full moon's light
dispenses silver round
the living room at night,
you step without a sound
among its gifts –

the glass, the brilliant doors
wide open everywhere
you go, the kitchen floor's
sea frozen solid, there,
beneath your feet

– and then you step outside.
You do not feel the chill.
Trees fizzing like the tide
above your head, but still
you do not wake.

You walk miles in your sleep
but still you do not wake.
You pass the park, the deep
waters of its boating lake,
the silent shops.

In bed, we think of you
out there, in all that space.
Your bare feet wet with dew.
The moonlight on your face.
So many stars.

If only you could see
those stars! They radiate
for all eternity
for you, although it's late
and you are far

away.

# The Sleepwalkers' Ball

When they arrive – alone, from all
four corners of the night,
travelling through empty streets
in nighties and pyjamas
thin as mist, through dark streets
dark enough for any ghosts
who have to dwell outside

– they shuffle in, in ones and twos,
down corridors made for ghosts . . .
cobwebs, mice, a squeaky door
 . . . then wait for bird-like butlers
to open every door.
The rooms are packed with dishes
white as drifts of snow.

No cakes exist, no crisps, no
vol-au-vents, just dishes
filled with air from draughty rooms
(but in their dreams there's ice cream
melting in sunlit rooms
where music plays). They dance,
they dance for hours and hours.

They've tousled hair and staring eyes
perhaps, but how they dance!
Their heads are full of music
so they dance in silence, through
the night. Cello music.
Saxophones. It makes them laugh.
The harps, the violins.

They dance until it's dawn,
then, leaving with a final laugh,
drift into the daylight
fast asleep, to head for home . . .
And later, in the brilliant light,
they wake to wonder how
their feet became so black.

# The Octopus
# Factory Night-Shift Girls

For hours on end we stand alone
in water that reaches our knees,
and when it splashes, we groan
or sigh: we chatter: we freeze.

Waves lap the one, long bench
at which we work all night.
To stop them rattling, we clench
our teeth. Our hands are white,

so white they look like fish . . .
cold hands no ordinary boy
will hold. (But we can wish.)
– What creatures we destroy!

Pike. Basking Shark. Crab. Ray.
We pare, we peel, we cut
the nasty bits away.
Piranha. Eel. Cod. Halibut.

Octopuses are the worst
by far: the way they flail
and flap before they burst,
before their poor hearts fail.

Our eyes water, our ears ring
when tentacles slap cheeks
so hard it's bound to sting.
Sometimes, for weeks.

For hours on end we dream
of blazing holidays inland
where the only stream
is a stream of boys, where sand

extends for miles and miles
in all directions, and palm trees
grown for shade, in aisles,
sway in a southerly breeze.

The breeze plays with our hair.
We shield our eyes from the sun.
The sun shines everywhere,
on everything and everyone

while suntanned waiters dispel
the heat with lemon iced tea.
What makes us grin so happily?
Well, in this dream we smell

absolutely nothing like the sea.

# My Last Castle

When no one was about
last night, I visited the sea:
small waves disintegrated on the beach
in front of me.

The gulls were packed away
somewhere, the tide was almost high;
it held aloft its little lamps of surf
and they broke with a sigh.

The moon was out.
I built a castle by its light
where the sand was not quite wet and not quite dry.
The battlements were bright,

their shadows deep and long.
I'm old (I thought) I'm much too old
for this, and the water was whispering to me
and it was cold.

I dug a moat
until it filled with sea, then crowned
the towers with lollipop sticks.
The only sound

was me (my breath)
and the regiments of winter waves
no one in their right mind
braves.

I left my castle there
last night, among the shells
I didn't use, I left my footprints
filling up like tiny wells

and, walking back,
I was lonely, yes, it's true,
and saddened even then, by what
the sea is made to do.

# Hide and Seek

You lose your father after dark
one Saturday, somewhere between
        home and Singleton Park.

Huge cars roar past: you've never seen
        shapes that black, eyes that bright.
Where will they go? Where have they been?

        Your dad's nowhere in sight
and yet you never closed your eyes.
        Now you are deep inside the night –

though night is only morning in disguise
        – and every street light stares
at you, or soaks you in its dyes.

        You're out alone, but no one cares . . .
and then you hear the paws, the steamy breath
        of wolves, of grizzly bears.

# The Paper Boys

Lonely in the moments before it's light,
the milkman's cart is humming to itself
past Nottage Lane, beyond the pub

as peaceful now as it has ever been,
through still estates towards the sea.

The pavements shine with last night's rain.

Too heavy to stand up straight, the trees
baptize us when we walk beneath them.
These streets belong to paper boys.

Carrying the news from door to door, we fold
the world then slip it through each letter box.

Curtains drawn, no one sees us when we pass

but the lightest sleepers hear our footsteps –
we enter their heads to occupy their dreams,
haunting the quiet roads at dawn.

Before the sky is anything but grey, we leave
an open gate, a barking dog, an empty bag

abandoned in a porch.

# Index of first lines